BEARMAN

BEARMAN

Exploring the World of Black Bears

LAURENCE PRINGLE

PHOTOGRAPHS BY
LYNN ROGERS

CHARLES SCRIBNER'S SONS • NEW YORK

For Rebecca Anne Pringle

Copyright © 1989 by Laurence Pringle
Illustrations copyright © 1989 by Lynn Rogers

Charles Scribner's Sons Books for Young Readers
Macmillan Publishing Company
866 Third Avenue, New York, NY 10022
Collier Macmillan Canada, Inc.

Printed in Hong Kong
First Edition   10   9   8   7   6   5   4   3   2   1

Library of Congress Cataloging-in-Publication Data
Pringle, Laurence P.   Bearman : exploring the world of black bears.
Bibliography: p.   Includes index.
Summary: Examines, in text and photographs, the physical characteristics, habits, and natural environment of the American black bear.
1. Black bear—Juvenile literature. [1. Black bear. 2. Bears]
I. Rogers, Lynn, ill.   II. Title.
QL737.C27P75   1989   599.74'446   89–5890   ISBN 0–684–19094–X

Grateful acknowledgment is made to Adelbert Rogers for use of the photographs on pages 3 and 5; to Greg Wilker for those on pages 10, 29, 35, and 36; and to Donna Rogers for those on pages 12 and 32.

CONTENTS

ONE

Becoming a Bearman

Lynn Rogers waited quietly as the bears approached. There were three of them—two cubs and their two-hundred-fifty-pound mother. Sniffing for food on the forest floor, the bears drew closer and closer.

Just fifty feet away, the mother bear caught the scent of a human. She turned and saw Lynn Rogers. Her ears bent back and flattened against her head. The great bear seemed about to attack.

Lynn Rogers stood still and waited. The bear lunged toward him. *Whoosh!* She let out an explosion of air as she slammed her front feet on the ground and came to a sudden stop. She turned away. She charged again but once more halted a few feet away. Then the huge bear turned and quickly led her cubs off through the woods.

Face-to-face with this bear, most people would have run for their lives. But Lynn Rogers, a United States Forest Service biologist, had studied black bears for more than twenty years. He knew that the mother's behavior was a bluff, a show to scare him away. Furthermore, Lynn Rogers knew the bear and her cubs intimately. He had observed them in the wild many times. The preceding winter he had crawled right into their den. He had hauled them out and weighed and measured each bear. While the mother was immobilized by a drug, he had fitted her with a radio-transmitter collar that she now wore around her neck.

On this day, signals from that radio had led him close to the bear and her cubs. Now he could pick up the antenna that lay on the ground nearby and soon locate the bear family again. But first he paused and made some notes about the encounter that had just occurred.

A patch of dense hazel brush grew nearby, and the Minnesota forest looked a bit like a tropical jungle. Lynn chuckled as he was reminded of his childhood and of how he had become a "bearman" who has devoted his adult life to learning about black bears.

Lynn Rogers was born in 1939, in Grand Rapids, Michigan, and was raised on the outskirts of that city. His parents were devout Baptists. At the age of seven, Lynn surprised them by saying he wanted to be a missionary when he grew up. His career goal had little to do with religion. Lynn loved the outdoors and figured that missionary work would take him to jungles full of wild animals.

"My mother encouraged my interest in nature," Lynn recalls. "When I was just two or three years old, she began to keep a scrapbook of pictures and articles about wildlife. She also fostered my curiosity about nature. I was sick with bronchitis a lot until my teenage years. I missed many schooldays and had to stay indoors. One thing that made those days more bearable was having books about birds and looking out a window at the birds that came to feed in our mulberry tree."

In the seventh grade Lynn wrote a theme about wildlife biologists. He was delighted to know that there were "people who actually worked in the woods and worked with wildlife."

By then his health was improving. With friends in the neighborhood he played football, basketball, softball. In the summer he rode his bike to nearby lakes to swim. A Sunday-school teacher introduced Lynn

2

Seven-year-old Lynn Rogers loved the outdoors.

to trout fishing. His passion for being outdoors grew. "Depending on the season, many days after school I was out either fishing or hunting."

Lynn Rogers graduated from high school in 1957. He wanted to study wildlife biology at Michigan State University but couldn't afford to attend. He enrolled in Grand Rapids Junior College, majoring in biology. (He was also on the swimming team and was named to the Junior College All-American team.) When he graduated from junior col-

After his graduation from high school, Lynn's goal was to become a wildlife biologist.

lege in 1959, he needed more money in order to attend Michigan State and took a job delivering mail for the United States Post Office.

Lynn Rogers's goal of being a wildlife biologist seemed far away, but his curiosity about nature remained strong. Once his mail delivery route was complete each day, he was free to roam outdoors. He still fished and hunted, but his interest in nature began to deepen and change.

"I saw many dogs on my mail route. I observed their behavior and was aware of how wolflike it was because I had been reading books about wolves. About this time, in my early twenties, I began to lose interest in hunting and fishing. My mail route took me past a camera store each day. For several reasons, perhaps going back to that nature scrapbook my mother made, I became deeply interested in wildlife photography. I felt challenged trying to get good photographs of wild animals—from chickadees to bears."

Lynn Rogers saw a wild black bear for the first time when he was twenty. He already "knew" that they were big, mean, and dangerous. After all, his mother had read him the Sugar Creek Gang stories, in which, Lynn recalls, "all bears were portrayed as fearsome creatures."

Hunting magazines also encouraged the notion that all bears were fierce animals. So Lynn was scared when he saw his first black bear at a public campsite by the Two Hearted River in Michigan's Upper Peninsula. As Lynn and a friend drove up to their camp at night, they saw a bear with its head in their fish bucket, eating their catch.

"The bear ran, and I jumped from the car and ran after it, yelling. Very soon, though, I realized that I was alone in the woods, without a gun, and didn't know where the bear was. I turned and ran out of the woods as fast as I had come in."

Lynn wanted to take photographs of black bears and had an opportunity in the summer of 1966. On vacation from his mail-delivery job, he and a friend looked for a bear at the town dump near Grand Marais, Michigan. Now, dumps are not everyone's idea of an appealing vacation spot, but bears (and other kinds of wildlife) are attracted to the plentiful food that people throw away. In wild areas, garbage dumps sometimes provide evening entertainment as people come to watch black bears feed.

Lynn Rogers drove to the dump in daytime and found a large black bear emerging from the forest. He crept from the car with his camera,

When Lynn Rogers took this photo in 1966, he believed that black bears were highly dangerous animals.

determined to get his first closeup pictures of a wild bear. His friend stayed in the car. A man watching from another car assured Lynn's friend that he had a rifle and would shoot the bear if it attacked.

"Many people, myself included, believed that black bears were highly dangerous animals," Lynn recalls. "Fortunately, I had a chance to learn about the real bears."

That fall Lynn Rogers began full-time study of wildlife biology at Michigan State University. During his 1967 summer vacation he had an opportunity to get field experience: studying wild doves in New Mexico. Just after learning that this summer job was his, Lynn heard that a student aide was needed for another wildlife project: capturing black bears in Michigan. He won that job, bowed out of the dove project, and was soon in close contact with black bears every day—and on many nights.

Some bears were tipping over garbage cans by people's homes or scaring people while searching for food at campgrounds. Lynn's job was to help E. M. "El" Harger catch these "nuisance bears" alive and let them go in other areas of Michigan's Upper Peninsula. Traps were made of sections of road culvert. When a bear entered a trap and tugged on some bait, a door dropped shut behind it.

The bear could then be drugged to keep it immobile while Lynn and El Harger recorded information. They weighed and measured each bear and put a numbered tag in each ear so that the animal could be identified later if it was recaptured or killed by a hunter.

"I loved working with black bears," Lynn recalls. "The most bears anyone had caught in Michigan was twenty-eight in a previous summer. El Harger went on vacation and left me in charge. I caught twenty-eight in one month. I was so thankful for the opportunity to study black bears that I hustled from dawn to far after dark."

That summer Lynn was visited by Dr. Albert Erickson of the University of Minnesota. Erickson was the first bearman in North America;

A bear was captured when it crawled into a trap to tug at bait, causing the trap's door to fall shut.

he had pioneered techniques for catching black bears alive. Erickson encouraged Lynn to continue bear research in Minnesota. The following spring Lynn Rogers graduated with honors from Michigan State. That summer he and El Harger captured and released more than a hundred nuisance black bears in Michigan, and in the fall of 1968 he began graduate research in Minnesota.

"Black bears had been studied in Virginia, New York, many other states, and in Canada," says Lynn. "Biologists had learned a lot, but there were still plenty of unanswered questions, about black bears in the Upper Great Lakes region and about black bears in general.

"The live trapping and tagging I had done gave me a glimpse of the bears' lives during the summer season. I was eager to know more about their lives in all seasons."

8

TWO

Getting to Know Black Bears

The creature that Lynn Rogers set out to study is *Ursus americanus*, the American black bear. It once lived in all forested areas of North America. Today it still survives in at least twenty-three states and all Canadian provinces. In about a dozen states the black bear is plentiful enough that a hunting season is allowed.

Although some individuals grow to be monsters of more than 600 pounds, most adult males weigh between 150 and 550 pounds, and females between 90 and 300 pounds. Despite their large size, black bears are good climbers. Their claws are sharp and tightly curved, just right for grasping and digging into the bark of a tree.

Black bears also rip into rotting logs to dig out grubs, ants, and other insects. They locate these foods by scent and with acute close-range color vision. Black bears' hearing is more sensitive than that of humans. Sometimes they stand upright, the better to see, to hear, and to detect scents in the air.

Lynn Rogers began his field research in 1969 with the basic goal of

learning more about the black bear population in Minnesota: its numbers, density, age pattern, and causes of death. His main study area was in the northeastern corner of the state, in the Superior National Forest.

"I started taking blood samples from captured bears, and studies of the blood showed that most bears were in good health. I was catching, tagging, and releasing many bears. The number of tags sent in by hunters showed that people were the main cause of adult bear deaths. Besides being shot, some bears were hit by motor vehicles."

Minnesota's bear population seemed to be thriving. But Lynn Rogers had learned that, in Minnesota, an average of six years passes while a bear develops from birth to an adult capable of reproducing. Because of their long life cycle, he would need many years to learn more about black bears' social behavior and how it affected their numbers. Fortunately, the technique of attaching radio transmitters to wild animals was then being developed. Using this method, Lynn could easily locate and follow black bears in all seasons.

In the summer of 1969, Lynn began putting radio-transmitter collars on some bears, then releasing them. "At first this was very frustrating. The radios stopped sending signals within a few months—or even weeks. It took a year to solve the problem. Then I really began to radio-track bears."

During the first nine years of his research, from 1969 to 1977, Lynn Rogers fitted one hundred and six bears with radio collars. "My work was helped enormously by a basic fact of bear life in Minnesota—they hibernate for five to seven months each winter. This enabled me to locate their dens and replace their radio collars before the batteries wore out. In this way I was able to keep track of individual bears year after year."

Equally important, the winter sleep of bears enabled Lynn to learn about entire bear families. After using radio signals to find the den of an

Early in his career, Lynn Rogers never dreamed he would someday be able to observe wild black bears closely.

Lynn Rogers put radio-transmitter collars on captured bears and was then able to locate them in the wild.

adult female bear that had given birth, he could put identifying tags on the ears of her cubs. The following winter, signals from the mother's radio collar would lead him to her new den, where he would find her and the yearling bears. The yearlings were then big enough to be fitted with their own radio collars and could be tracked after they left their mother and struck out on their own. In this way, over a span of years Lynn was able to follow the lives of three or four generations of black bears.

There's adventure in radio-tracking wildlife, but there's also plenty of hard work. Lynn traveled over one hundred and twenty square miles of wilderness in all seasons. In summertime he drove, hiked, and canoed, and often had to be out at the peak season of biting flies and mosquitoes. In wintertime he traveled by snowmobile and on snow-shoes in temperatures that dropped far below zero. In all seasons Lynn Rogers sometimes flew in a light aircraft. He operated the antenna device to locate a radio-collared bear while the pilot followed directions so they could pinpoint its position. They survived two crash landings.

From the air Lynn saw bears traveling, feeding, and even chasing, fighting, and mating. He sometimes observed for several minutes as two evenly matched males clawed and bit one another, fighting for the

In the air or on the ground, Rogers found bears by detecting signals from the transmitters they carried.

During the winter, Lynn Rogers and his pilot used radio signals from bears to find their dens.

opportunity to mate with a female. Lynn also saw female bears defending their territories, chasing trespassing females away.

Once a bear den was located from the air, Lynn could reach it on the ground. Sometimes he and his assistants took turns hiding near a den and observed bears as they prepared their dens and as they emerged from them. In the spring, mothers with cubs usually stayed near their dens for about two weeks. Snow still covered most of the ground, there was little food available, and the bears did not roam far.

Lynn also observed that mother bears often led their cubs from their den to the base of a white pine tree—an easy tree for the cubs to climb in case of danger. Mother bears devoted themselves to the care of their cubs. Lynn Rogers said, "Nursing mothers seem almost human at times. One picture that sticks vividly in my mind is of a mother sitting with her back against a tree, cradling her cubs in her arms and licking the heads of the cubs nursing at her chest."

Rogers and his assistants traveled by snowmobile or on snowshoes to reach bear dens.

Cubs quickly climb trees when they sense danger.

Although Lynn was outdoors in all seasons, his research also involved many hours spent indoors, making sense of all the data he was gathering and writing of his findings for scientific journals. He plotted on maps the changing locations of individual bears. Since he was tracing the movements of as many as forty radio-collared bears at a time, he eventually learned a lot about their ranges, their longest treks, and where they found food at different times of the year.

Black bears need large amounts of fruit and nuts before going into hibernation, and often travel far in the late summer and fall for this food. Lynn Rogers calls this the fall foraging trip. The bears that Lynn Rogers followed usually moved southeast, closer to Lake Superior, where soil conditions often provided abundant food. The bears traveled farthest in years when food was scarce. The year 1976 was such a time, and one male bear that weighed four hundred and fifty pounds left its usual range in late July, then traveled one hundred and nineteen miles south before returning home to a den in late October. (The return trip took just nine days.)

Many bears fed at garbage dumps, especially when natural foods were scarce. Males in particular did so, and one seven-year-old male was tracked as it moved from one dump to another, the last one twenty-five miles from its normal home. Food from dumps allowed the bears to extend their vital fattening-up period just before hibernation. Usually several bears fed peacefully at a dump. However, when natural foods were scarce, Lynn Rogers observed that "fights at dumps were more frequent and severe."

By 1977, when Lynn Rogers received a doctoral degree from the University of Minnesota, he had learned a great deal about the social behavior of black bears and how it affected their travels and population. Black bears have what is called a matriarchal society: It is run by the mothers.

Cubs stay with their mother until they are about one and a half years old.

Each mother bear has a territory that averages nearly four square miles in size. Her cubs stay with her until they are yearlings, about seventeen months old. Then they begin to live in small ranges within their mother's territory. A year or two later the young males leave the area, sometimes traveling a hundred miles in search of a new range that overlaps the ranges of several females. The daughters usually stay near their mother and expand their ranges as they grow older. The mother avoids trespassing on the ranges of her young.

"This behavior," said Lynn Rogers, "aids yearling bears in getting their own exclusive feeding areas, and aids daughters in getting territories. When the bears wake up in the spring, they usually reestablish the same territories year after year. Sometimes female bears trespass on one

Bears often roam far from home on their fall foraging trip.

another's territory to steal food, and this can lead to chasing and occasional battles.

"I've never seen an actual fight between neighboring matriarchs, but one fine June day I caught two females, an eleven-year-old and a fourteen-year-old with cubs, and both had fresh puncture wounds and lacerations on their heads and necks. Although the eleven-year-old's wounds were more extensive, it was the fourteen-year-old mother and her cubs that later withdrew from the disputed area."

The adult males play a vital role, of course, in the June-July mating period, but then have no contact with the cubs they father and usually none with the mother bear until she is ready to mate again, two or more years later. Males live on the fringes of the territories that are maintained by mother bears.

A male bear follows a female in the summer mating season.

THREE

Inside Bear Dens

Black bears have sharp teeth and claws. They are big and powerful and can run faster than humans. They look capable of getting food by killing other animals. They *do* gobble down many creatures—ants—but feed mostly on berries, nuts, and other plant foods.

Since their diet is mostly easy-to-digest plant foods, the lives of black bears are strongly affected by the annual cycle of plant growth and fruiting. In the early spring, bears eat plant parts that are just beginning to grow: newly sprouted grass, opening buds and flowers. In late spring and early summer, black bears often get more than half of their food by ripping into logs for ant pupae and digging into nests of wasps and bees. Berries and nuts, available in the summer and fall, usually enable bears to store fat and other nutrients they need for their long winter sleep.

In some parts of North America black bears fatten up on acorns, hickory nuts, and beechnuts in autumn. Bears find little of this food in the evergreen forests of northern Minnesota. Lynn Rogers found that some bears traveled more than twenty miles to feast on the acorn crop of

Food is scarce when a bear first leaves its den in the spring.

a rare stand of oak trees. They also ate hazelnuts and the berries of mountain ash trees. When these natural foods became scarce, the bears prepared a den for the long, harsh winter ahead.

Both Lynn Rogers and Gary Alt, a bearman in Pennsylvania, have crawled into more bear dens than any other person and, for that matter, more than any single black bear. In the wild, a bear seldom lives more than a dozen years and uses a different den almost every year. As Lynn Rogers has pursued his curiosity about black bears, he has wriggled into more than two hundred dens.

It was vital for Lynn to find dens so he could keep functioning radio collars on many bears in order to continue to follow them. But he also wanted to learn about bear hibernation and how these large mammals survived the harsh Minnesota winters.

Black bears prefer hollow trees for dens but find few of these in

Most black bears depend on such plant foods as mountain ash berries, hazelnuts, and blueberries, rather than on meat or fish.

Lynn Rogers inspects a rock cave where a 455-pound male bear made its den.

northern Minnesota. So they spend the winter in rock caves or crevices, burrows, and hollows that they dig under fallen trees or brush piles. "For some unknown reason," said Lynn Rogers, "black bears seldom reuse a den, although an abandoned den may eventually be used by another bear. In one case, this behavior cost a bear its life. Rather than den in either of two safe, previously used caves in her territory, a pregnant fifteeen-year-old female built a poorly protected nest on the ground. Later that winter I discovered that she and her newborn cubs had been killed by a pack of wolves."

Usually a bear chooses its den site and prepares it before snow covers the ground. The bear stays near the den and becomes less and less active. It does, however, make a nest of cedar bark, leaves, evergreen boughs, or other materials before settling in for the winter. In 1972, as Lynn and two assistants watched, three cubs born the preceding winter tried to help their mother prepare a burrow under the roots of a fallen tree.

"The cubs raked leaves, grass, and forest litter, backing toward the den as they pulled piles of materials with their front paws. The five-year-old mother did the same. She also took charge of arranging all the nest material in the den. Twice she scooped everything out of the den, sending it flying backward between her legs and then putting it back her own way."

By late October nearly all bears in northeastern Minnesota have begun to hibernate. In the milder climate of southern states, bears may not hibernate until December or even January. Minnesota bears also go into a deeper hibernation than those that live in milder climates. The bears that Lynn Rogers studied seldom left their dens from late October to early April. Some especially fat bears entered dens as early as mid-September and slept for seven months.

Nesting materials protect the bear (and cubs) from the cold ground, and heavy snowfall helps close the entrance. In times of light snowfall, however, the den temperatures are about the same as outside—on some nights as low as 30 degrees Fahrenheit *below zero*.

"The main insulation for a bear," said Lynn Rogers, "is its fur, which is thickest on the back, neck, and sides and thinnest on the muzzle, legs, and underside. A hibernating bear sleeps in a curled-up position with its nose near its tail. This minimizes a bear's surface area and reduces heat loss from the thinly furred areas.

"One, two, or three cubs are born in January. They weigh less than a pound and have practically no hair at first. After giving birth the

25

Lynn called this bear Wilma. She was fourteen years old when she gave birth to these three cubs.

mother resumes her deep sleep, but she wakes up occasionally and tends to the cubs' needs. The cubs do not hibernate. They suckle and sleep snuggled warmly against their mother's sparsely furred underside. By the time they leave the den, at three months of age, they weigh between four and eight pounds."

Lynn Rogers calls black bears "masters of winter survival." They sleep for months without eating, drinking, urinating, or defecating. Such hibernators as chipmunks and woodchucks cannot do this; even though their body temperature may drop below 40 degrees Fahrenheit, they must occasionally warm up and awaken and rid themselves of wastes. Sometimes they eat. Black bears, with their well-insulated pelts and large size, lose body heat very slowly. Their temperature stays above 88 degrees, within 12 degrees of their summer temperature. This enables black bears to arouse themselves and react to danger faster than other hibernators.

"Most of the bears I visited in dens were wakeful enough to lift their heads and look at me. However, one March day I accidentally fell on a female in her den. She didn't wake up for at least eight minutes even though her cubs bawled loudly and I began gently prodding her."

The heart rate of a hibernating bear tends to vary, increasing to forty beats a minute at times and dropping to just eight beats a minute at other times. Lynn Rogers listens for the heartbeat at a den entrance.

"On calm days I can hear the rapid, strong heartbeat of alert bears, but I can't hear the heartbeat of bears in deep hibernation sleep. Once I crawled into the den of a soundly sleeping bear and pressed my ear against her chest. I couldn't hear anything. After about two minutes, though, I suddenly heard a strong, rapid heartbeat. The bear was waking up. Within a few seconds she lifted her head as I tried to squeeze backward through the den entrance. Outside, I could still hear the heartbeat, which I timed at about 175 beats per minute. This heart rate during arousal from hibernation is even higher than rates that have been measured for very active bears."

Toward the end of winter, in March, Lynn Rogers and his assistants visit all dens to gather data on the bears, tag young cubs' ears, and replace batteries of radio transmitters. With a hypodermic needle on the end of a stick he jabs an immobilizing drug into the muscles of the adult bear. Within fifteen minutes or so the bear can be hauled out to be examined and weighed. Yearling bears get their first radio collars. Cubs, which are wide awake, are also weighed and examined.

"To protect the cubs from cold," said Lynn Rogers, "we often tuck them right inside our shirts or coats, near the warmth of our bodies. Sometimes they make the same 'comfort sound'—like the combination of a purr and an engine—that they make when they are nursing. After we put the mother back in the den, we put the cubs on her chest so they can nurse. Then we cover the entrance of the den with snow and try to get away before she wakes up."

At den entrances, Rogers could often hear the contented sounds of nursing cubs and the mother bear's heartbeat.

The March weight of a cub or yearling tells a lot about its chances for survival. At one den, for example, Lynn weighed two yearling bears: The male weighed twenty-five pounds, the female seventeen.

"She's too light," he said. "Yearlings that weigh less than twenty pounds have only about a fifty-fifty chance of surviving the next few months. Underweight cubs also may starve in the spring and early summer. However, adult bears somehow struggle through, even though a nursing mother may lose as much as forty percent of her weight during the winter.

"Back in the mid-1970s we had poor crops of wild berries and nuts for three years in a row. Not only did a lot of cubs and yearlings die, but some mature female bears failed to reproduce."

Lynn Rogers and his wife, Donna, weigh a three-year-old female.

Having enough suitable habitat is vital for the survival of all wild animals, including black bears. The research of Lynn Rogers, his assistants, and other bearmen has given wildlife biologists and foresters useful information about the needs of black bears. "Here in northern Minnesota," said Lynn Rogers, "food is the key to a thriving bear popu-

Colleen Rogers keeps a cub warm until it and its mother are returned to their den.

lation. So foresters should avoid cutting stands of oak and other food-producing trees and should encourage growth of wild berries."

Some knowledge from black bear studies may benefit humans. Blood samples taken from hibernating bears by Lynn Rogers have been found to have high levels of cholesterol. In fact, hibernating bears often have cholesterol levels more than twice those of most people. Neverthe-

A well-fed cub that weighs five pounds or more in the spring is off to a good start toward adulthood.

less, this cholesterol causes no known health problems in bears, as it does in humans.

Medical researchers are trying to learn more about this and about how black bears stay so healthy during their long winter sleep. The information that Lynn Rogers and others have gained from crawling into bear dens may someday lead to the production of better medicines for people.

Lynn Rogers examines a bear that weighed 611 pounds in the fall and 475 pounds after its long winter sleep.

FOUR

The Most Exciting Animal in the Woods

In 1988 Lynn Rogers said, "I've learned more about bear behavior in the last few years than in all of my previous years of research."

This was quite a statement, considering what he had learned in previous years. Since 1976 he has studied black bears for the United States Forest Service's North Central Forest Experiment Station, aided by as many as a dozen assistants in the summertime. The knowledge gained about black bears has been published in more than sixty scientific reports, including a 1987 monograph published by The Wildlife Society.

In the mid-1980s, Lynn Rogers's research turned in a new direction. "We had learned a lot about the travels of bears; for example, that a certain individual was at point A one day and at point B on another. And sometimes we could see the bear from the airplane. All too often, though, the bear was hidden by vegetation. What was it doing? I wished we could observe wild bears more closely."

That seemed unlikely, since bears usually run away from people.

Wild black bears usually do their best to avoid people.

However, in the summer of 1984 a bear began to look for food at the North Central Experiment Station laboratory that is Lynn Rogers's headquarters. Lynn decided to use food to help the bear be less afraid of him. That bear (and others that came later) loved bits of fat from a supermarket meat department. It grew accustomed to the presence of Lynn Rogers. However, it fled whenever Lynn approached it in the woods.

"This was discouraging," Lynn recalled, "but I continued to provide tasty morsels for bears the following summer." In the summer of 1985, supplies of wild berries and nuts were very low. As many as eighteen bears visited the research lab for bits of food. (In contrast, natural food was so abundant in 1988 that only one bear appeared.) Several of these bears became accustomed to the presence of Lynn Rogers and his assistants.

Once bears became accustomed to Lynn's presence, they ignored him and went about their normal activities.

Eventually, Lynn and his assistants were able to travel and rest with certain bears for a day or two at a time.

"I was amazed by the way the bears ignored me. A mother would leave her cubs right beside me and chase away another female. There were fights and chases nearby, but I was not viewed as a threat. A bear's greatest fear is another bear, and they acted as though I wasn't there.

"I thought, if only the bears would continue to treat me like 'the invisible man' in the wild. That fall we had our first clue that this might be possible."

Research assistant Greg Wilker used radio signals to find the den of bear number 401, a female that had sometimes visited the lab for food. Greg found 401 resting outside her den, and she did not flee when he approached, nor when Lynn visited a day later. The following spring, 401 started to run when Greg approached, but stopped. Before long, Lynn Rogers and his assistants were accompanying 401 on her daily, and nightly, routine. Working in twelve-hour shifts, Greg and another research assistant, Charlie Cowden, routinely stayed with the bear for twenty-four or even forty-eight hours in a row. Eventually, 401's younger sisters, Patch and Terry, were also closely followed by the bearmen.

"The bears ignore us, even though we may be only a few feet away," said Lynn Rogers. "If a bear rips into a stump for ants, we can literally step up and look over its shoulder. The bears take naps, nurse their cubs, and play as if we're not there."

At first the biologists jotted down their observations on paper. Now they use a laptop computer to quickly record data about the bear's activities, right down to the number of bites it takes of its food.

"There are questions about bears that I never thought I'd get

A black bear rips into a log for ant pupae, a favorite spring and summer food.

A black bear's threatening look may lead to a scary but harmless bluff charge.

answers to, but close following of a few bears has begun to give us those answers. We are learning more about bear communication, about how they use the forest, how they respond to weather, what and how much they eat, and what kinds of habitat they use for different activities."

Lynn Rogers's recent, closeup work with bears has also changed a notion about them that he learned as a child. "Even though I had never been hurt by a bear, I still felt, deep down, that they were dangerous. As recently as 1984, I met a bear in the woods and it came at me. It lunged, stopped, smacked down a bush. I let it be, feeling I had been in danger.

"I now realize that I could have kept following that bear. Tagging along with 401 and other bears has taught me this: What looks and sounds like an attack is a display that means, 'Get back, I'm uneasy with you.' It is called a *bluff charge*."

A bear usually blows out some air before making this charge, and lets out a giant *whoosh* when it stops. On one occasion, a bear did not stop charging. Lynn stepped back quickly, tripped, fell down. The bear stood over him for a few seconds, then ran away. It never made a sound. Judging from reports from people who have actually been hurt by black bears, a silent charging bear is more likely to be dangerous than one making scary noises.

A few people have been killed or injured by black bears. However, considering how often people and bears are in close contact at national parks, campgrounds, and garbage dumps, the numbers are low. For every human killed by a black bear in North America, about twelve die from spider bites and twenty from snake bites. Lynn Rogers urges people to respect black bears, to keep a distance from them, but also to stop thinking of them as highly dangerous animals.

Many people find bears appealing. They are like humans in several ways: about our size, able to stand and walk on the soles of their feet, committed to extended care of their young. Black bears are also especially intelligent mammals.

Kelly Rogers met Patch when the bear was a yearling.

More than before, Lynn Rogers's recent studies have enabled him to know some bears as individuals. "It is easy to feel attached to them. We get to know them so well, and each has a distinct personality. When one of these bears dies, it feels like [we're] losing a close friend."

Several have died. In 1987, bear number 401 was killed by another bear. And in September of 1988, Patch was shot by a hunter while she was on her fall foraging trip.

Lynn Rogers will continue to follow Terry, and perhaps the offspring of Patch. He still feels that black bears are the most exciting animals in the woods. And he feels lucky to be in the forest with the bears, learning about their lives.

FURTHER READING

Alt, Gary, and J. M. Gruttaduria. "Reuse of Black Bear Dens in Northeastern Pennsylvania." *Journal of Wildlife Management*, vol. 48, no. 1 (1984), pp. 236–239.

Conover, Adele. "Getting to Know Black Bears—Right on Their Own Home Ground." *Smithsonian*, April 1983, pp. 86–97.

Fair, Jeffrey. *The Great American Black Bear*. Minocqua, Wisconsin: North Word Press, 1989 (color photos by Lynn Rogers).

Herrero, Steven. *Bear Attacks: Their Causes and Avoidance*. Piscataway, N.J.: Nick Lyons Books, 1985.

Pelton, M. R. "Black Bear." J. A. Chapman and G. A. Feldhammer, editors, *Wild Mammals of North America: Biology, Management, and Economics, pp. 504–514*. Baltimore: The Johns Hopkins Press, 1982.

Rogers, Lynn. "A Bear in Its Lair." *Natural History*, October 1981, pp. 64–70.

————."Effects of Food Supply and Kinship on Social Behavior, Movements, and Population Growth of Black Bears in Northeastern Minnesota." Wildlife Monograph number 97. Bethesda, Maryland: The Wildlife Society, 1987.

————."Effects of Mast and Berry Crop Failures on Survival, Growth, and Reproductive Success of Black Bears." *Transactions of the 41st North American Wildlife and Natural Resources Conference*. Washington, D.C.: The Wildlife Management Institute, 1976.

————."Homing by Radio-Collared Black Bears, *Ursus americanus*, in Minnesota." *The Canadian Field-Naturalist*, fall 1986, pp. 350–353.

————."The Ubiquitous American Black Bear." William Nesbitt and Jack Parker, editors, *North American Big Game*, pp. 28–33. Washington, D.C.: The Boone and Crockett Club and the National Rifle Association of America, 1977.

Steinhart, P. "Getting to Know Bruin Better." *National Wildlife*, June–July 1978, pp. 20–27.

INDEX